Good HUNTING for Kids

Allen Morris Jones

Copyright © 2025 by Allen Morris Jones

ISBN-13: 978-0-9961560-8-0

Manufactured in the United States of America

All rights reserved. With the exception of short excerpts used for promotional, review, or academic purposes, no portion of this work may be reproduced or distributed in print or electronic form without the written permission of the publisher.

Published in the United States by

Bangtail Press
P.O. Box 11262
Bozeman, MT 59719

www.bangtailpress.com

For Corey, Morgan, Baylee, Kasey, and all the kids who hunt.

Why Hunt?

Hunting is one of the healthiest and most amazing things you can do in the outdoors. When you hunt, you're learning how the world smells and feels. You're learning about wild animals and how they behave. And you're learning about yourself, about how far you can walk and how long you can stand in one place, waiting. You're learning about your own body and how it reacts to buck fever, how your heart beats faster and your hands tremble. You're learning about your food and where it comes from.

It wasn't all that long ago that almost everybody in the world hunted. If you wanted to eat meat, you had to either raise it yourself or go out and hunt it. Humans and our ancestors hunted for millions of years. It's how we evolved. But very few people today know how to hunt, and

quite a few people really dislike it. That might be because they haven't gone out and tried it for themselves. If they had, they would know how *right* it feels. They would know that it's only when we're hunting that certain pieces of the world start to make sense.

It's a very serious thing, though, trying to hunt and kill another living creature. You're lucky to get to do it, but it's important to do it well. Which is what this book is for. It's meant to give you some helpful hints, some tips and tricks, and maybe give you something to think about along the way.

There are so many ways to be a hunter. We should all try to be the best hunters that we can be!

Safety First

When you first learn to hunt, it will be so exciting and fun that it will be easy to forget what a big responsibility it is. If you're not careful, the tool in your hands—whether it's a rifle, shotgun, or bow—can hurt or even kill you or another person. Never forget that.

To be a good hunter, you need to always keep at least four rules in mind. Learn them and remember them so that they become second nature. You should know them so well that you don't even have to think about them.

Number One

Treat every gun like it's loaded. This is so important. When accidents happen, it's often because somebody thought their gun was safely unloaded.

Number Two

Always point the gun away from people and in a safe direction, usually at the ground.

Number Three

Keep your finger off the trigger until you're ready to shoot. In fact, keep your finger entirely outside the trigger guard.

Number Four

Know what your target is and what's behind it. Don't ever shoot if you don't know where the bullet is going to land.

Bonus Rule

Never, ever, EVER let your friends handle your gun, not unless you're sure they already know what they're doing.

Good Hunting

If you want to be a good hunter, you will need to be able to do more than walk quietly in the woods and shoot safely and well, although you should be able to do those things, too. Being a good hunter means being a part of something larger than yourself. It means paying attention to which way the wind is blowing and knowing if the animals will be able to smell you. It means looking at tracks and knowing what kinds of animals made them, and what they were doing at the time. Were they hunting or playing or running? And most of all, maybe, it means being grateful that you get to spend time in nature chasing these animals. It's pretty easy to be a *good* hunter. To be a *great* hunter, though, takes a whole lifetime.

Rifle, Bow, or Shotgun?

Hunting for big game animals is usually done with either a rifle or a bow. Some people will also use shotguns. Rifles shoot farther and more accurately than bows or shotguns. They're also less likely to wound an animal, so they're probably the best thing for beginners to use.

Bowhunting is harder, but it can also be more rewarding. To do it well, you'll need to work harder, practice more, and be more skilled in the woods.

Rifles come in different calibers, or bullet sizes. Bigger animals need bigger calibers. Most rifles also have scopes on them. Scopes are sights that magnify your target, making it easier to shoot accurately.

Shotguns are good for close-range shooting, especially in brush or heavy timber. If you're deer hunting with a shotgun, you'll likely use a slug, which is a heavy type of ammunition.

It's important that you take your rifle, bow, or shotgun to the range to practice. A lot. When you release an arrow or squeeze the trigger, you owe it to the animal to make a good shot. There is nothing worse than the feeling that you made an animal suffer because you didn't practice enough.

Small Game

Before you hunt big game or birds, you'll probably start plinking around with a BB gun, shooting at tin cans or paper targets. And after a BB gun, you might graduate to a .22 rifle. This is a big step. A .22 is a small caliber, but it's still a lot of responsibility.

With a .22, or maybe a small shotgun like a .410, you can start hunting small game. This is an important step in learning how to be a good hunter. A lot of very skilled hunters started out by hunting squirrels or rabbits.

As you hunt small game, please remember that these are still living creatures. You need to be respectful as you hunt them. After you shoot them, one way to show respect is to eat them. Eating what you kill is an important part of being a good hunter. In the old days, our grandparents and great-grandparents had very good recipes for squirrels and rabbits!

Choosing a Bow

If you decide to go bowhunting, there are a few different types of bows you can use.

Most hunters use compound bows. These bows have wheels, or cams. The cams make it easier to pull back and hold at full draw. If you see an animal coming, you can draw the bow while you're still hidden and then wait for it to step out into the open. This is a big advantage.

Recurve bows are simpler, but not as strong, and it's harder to hold them at full draw. You also need to be closer to the animal. Recurves have a little bit of a curve to the body of the bow.

Longbows are basically straight sticks. They're not as strong or as accurate as other bows. Still, some of the best hunters like to use them. You need to be very close to the animal to be able to make a shot. Longbows are a real challenge!

Woodcraft

To be the best hunter you can be, you're going to need to learn some woodcraft. You'll need to know not only how to track, but also what sort of animal made a certain pile of scat (or poop). You'll need to learn how well certain animals can see in the dark, and how keen their sense of smell is. Do elk pay attention to deer when the deer run from you? How far does sound travel when you step on a dry stick? Most of all, you will need to just sit and watch the animals when they don't know you're around. This is how you'll learn how they behave.

Some of this can be read in books, but most of it you'll pick up from just spending a lot of time in the outdoors, tracking and watching and paying attention. If you're very lucky, you might also know an experienced hunter who can teach you some woodcraft.

Shot Placement

Part of being a good hunter is knowing when to take a shot and where on the animal's body to aim. This is very important. If you shoot in the wrong place, you could badly wound the animal without killing it right away.

You'll want to shoot in the lungs or heart. The best shots are often broadside, when the animal is walking across your field of vision. If the animal is walking straight toward you or straight away, you should probably pass on the shot. When the animal is broadside, its shoulder blade will cover some of its chest. It's a good idea to aim at the top of the crease where its front leg meets the chest. This is about where the top of its heart is, as well as the lungs.

If you're uncertain at all, if your aim is wobbly, or if the animal's moving too fast, you might want to wait for another shot. It's much better to let an animal get away than to wound it.

Below, the deer's lungs are pink, the heart is red, and the shoulder and leg bones are pale brown. You should aim for the pink or red.

> Whitetail antlers, top, branch off the main beam. Mule deer antlers split.

Types of Deer

There are a few different kinds of deer in North America that you can hunt. Most people hunt either mule deer in the West or whitetail deer almost everywhere. Whitetails often like thick brush. You'll find them along river and creek bottoms or sometimes, in the West, in heavy pine timber. They have smaller ears, browner bodies, and tails that wave like white flags when they run away. The bucks have antlers with points that branch off the curve of the main beam.

Mule deer usually prefer higher, drier country. They have large ears, grayer bodies, and small tails with black tips. The bucks have antlers with a main beam that splits into halves.

Whitetail Deer

Whitetail deer like places with heavy brush where they can hide. Whitetails are *really* good at hiding. For this reason, they're almost always best hunted slowly. Instead of covering lots of ground like you might for mule deer, you should find a place where you know there are deer and get there just before sunrise or not long before dark. Start slipping through the trees and brush. Be as quiet as you can. Or, better yet, find a trail that whitetails like to use and set up a ground blind or a treestand close by. Treestands are like little tree houses or platforms where you can sit and wait for a deer to show itself. It takes a lot of patience, but it's also very rewarding. You get to sit and watch birds and squirrels go about their day. The biggest whitetail bucks got that way because they're good at outsmarting hunters. You need to be even smarter!

Mule Deer

Hunting mule deer usually means a lot of walking. You'll want to stay off the ridgelines and use your binoculars to try and spot the deer before they see you. And no matter how careful you are, the biggest bucks will somehow almost always see you before you see them.

Mule deer and whitetails both rut in the fall. The rut is that time of year when the bucks chase the does. Bucks become so interested in does that even the smartest ones don't pay as much attention to people. This is a good time to hunt for a really big buck! The peak of the rut is influenced by weather (colder is better, stormy is better), but it usually happens in November.

It might be a temptation to hunt mule deer from a warm truck, but this is not ethical. The best hunters walk and work for it, giving the animals a chance to smell them and see them and outsmart them!

Rocky Mountain Elk

There are several species of elk in North America, but the most familiar—and the one you're most likely to hunt—is the Rocky Mountain elk.

In September and early October, elk will gather together in herds. This is when the bulls bugle and fight, and this is when you can bowhunt for them. You can sometimes bugle like a bull elk and get a bull to respond. If you're very lucky, the bull might even come in close, looking for a fight. There are few things as exciting as seeing a big bull elk charge in toward your bugle.

In late October and November, the bulls and cows go their separate ways again. If you're in the mountains and there's a lot of snow on the ground, you can sometimes hunt elk based on how they move up and down the mountain. You can predict their movements. The more snow there is up high, the more likely they are to be found lower down, near the valley floor.

Elk will always need three things: thick cover, good food, and access to water. If you can find places in elk country that have all three, then there might be elk nearby.

Pronghorn Antelope

Antelope like flat, wide-open country. The flatter the better and the more open the better. That's because they have really good eyesight. They feel most comfortable when they can see a long way. If you're hunting antelope, be prepared to walk a lot and use your binoculars. When hunters use their binoculars, it's called glassing.

Antelope can be easy to find but hard to get close to. If you antelope hunt, you might spend a lot of time stalking rather than just walking.

Antelope are very curious, too. Years ago, hunters used to lure them in close just by holding up a flag and letting it flap. The antelope just *had* to come up close to see what was going on. These days, that trick probably wouldn't work, but some bowhunters still use decoys that look like other antelope in order to draw them in close.

Buck antelope have black faces, while doe antelope do not. If you want to tell bucks from does at a distance, look for black noses.

Bighorn Sheep

One of the most exciting animals to hunt is the bighorn sheep. They're hard to hunt, though. Not just because they live in wild, steep places, but also because it's tough to get a permit.

In order to hunt bighorns, you usually have to either pay a lot of money to an outfitter or put your name into a lottery drawing. If you're very, very lucky, you'll see one of the tags arrive in the mail.

Bighorns rut in late November and December. This is when the rams come together with the ewes, which makes them easier to find. If you hunt them earlier, the big rams will usually be off by themselves in bachelor groups. The trick is to find where they're hiding. If you have a tag, you should scout the area where they live and then make a plan.

There are other types of sheep in North America as well, including Dall sheep (the white ones), stone sheep, and desert bighorns.

Mountain Goats

Mountain goats mostly live above timberline in the high peaks of the Rockies and in Alaska. They're nimble and surefooted, and feel safest up in the cliffs where predators are afraid to go.

Like bighorn sheep, to hunt goats, you either need to pay a lot of money to an outfitter or draw a tag. These permits are easier to get than sheep tags, though. Not much easier, but a little.

Once you have a permit, the work begins. You need to climb high into the peaks and spend a lot of time with binoculars, glassing. This is amazing country. You'll feel lucky just to be able to spend time there.

It's hard to tell male goats (billies) from female goats (nannies). You'll probably end up judging mostly based on body size. To be able to do that, you'll need to look at quite a few goats.

Before you shoot, be sure you know where the goat will fall. You don't want to risk your life trying to get to your goat if it falls in the middle of a treacherous cliff.

Black Bears

There are a few different kinds of bears in North America, but most hunters are interested in black bears. If you're black bear hunting in the Northern Rockies, though, you also need to know what grizzly bears look like—if only so you can avoid them and not accidentally shoot one.

Black bears aren't always black. Sometimes they're brown, like grizzlies, or red or even a little blondish. Black bears don't have a shoulder hump, and they have a flatter, Roman-nose kind of face.

To hunt black bears in the mountains, you will probably do a lot of walking in the spring or fall. You should find a high place with a good view of open parks in the trees. At sunrise or sunset, you'll use your binoculars to look for bears out grazing in the open. Bears like to eat grass, believe it or not, and you'll sometimes see them out feeding almost like deer or elk.

After you kill your bear, you'll probably want the hide for a rug or a mount. It's important to treat it well. You won't want to drag the bear like you might drag a deer or elk.

If you eat the bear, make sure the meat is cooked very well. Bears can carry a parasite called trichinosis, which can make you sick.

Moose and Caribou

Some of the most interesting and adventurous hunting can be found in the far north. And two of the most exciting animals to hunt in the north are moose and caribou.

Moose are big animals, but they can be surprisingly hard to spot. If you're hunting in the northern tundra, you might spend hours glassing and not seeing anything at all. But then suddenly, a huge bull moose will appear, the shovels of its antlers shining in the sun.

Moose rut in the fall, and this is when the bulls can sometimes be

called in. Be careful, though. Moose can be dangerous. Some people say that a cow moose with a calf is one of the most dangerous animals you can encounter.

Caribou are known for migrating in huge herds in the fall and spring. Thousands of them come together before moving toward better forage. But when it's time to hunt them in late summer or early fall, you might find the bulls off by themselves. Sometimes you'll see them lying out on glaciers and snow fields, just trying to escape the ferocious mosquitoes.

Pheasants and Grouse

When it comes to bird hunting, there are three main types: waterfowl hunting (ducks and geese), upland hunting (most everything else), and turkey hunting.

Bird hunting usually means using a shotgun, which is very different from using a rifle or a bow. It's hard to get used to shooting at flying objects. Most people start by practicing at the range, shooting trap or skeet.

Pheasants are especially fun to hunt. They're also tasty to eat. They like bottomlands and grainfields with good cover. You might be walking and walking and walking, and then birds will suddenly flush up from under your feet, scaring the pants off of you! Be sure you only shoot the rooster pheasants, though. They're the colorful ones.

Pheasants, left, ruffed grouse, center, and Hungarian partridge, right, are just a few of the upland birds you can hunt.

People also hunt grouse. There are lots of different species of grouse. In the mountains, there are blue grouse (or dusky grouse), ruffed grouse, and spruce grouse. On the prairie, there are sharp-tailed grouse and sage grouse. In the east, it's mostly ruffed grouse. If you're going grouse hunting, expect to do a lot of walking. Even when the birds are plentiful, once you start looking for them, they'll have somehow all disappeared. But most grouse are really good to eat, and when you do finally shoot one, it will feel like you really earned it!

Hungarian partridge are also fun to hunt. They like to stay together in flocks. If you flush up a bunch of Huns, they'll fly a little ways and then coast back down to the ground. You might have a chance to follow up and flush them again.

Depending on where you live, you can also hunt quail, chukars, woodcock, snipe, and doves.

Turkeys

Turkey hunting has more in common with elk and deer hunting than it does with other kinds of bird hunting. You don't flush turkeys or decoy them the way you do with ducks and geese. Instead, in the spring, you try to locate them, and then you hide and make the sound of a gobbling male turkey, or a tom. Hopefully, a bird will gobble back. If you are really well camouflaged and if you set up downwind, you might get to see a big tom come strutting through the woods toward you. The tom may spread its feathers and puff up and parade around.

There are five different kinds of turkeys in North America. The Eastern wild turkey is the most common; it's found in 38 states. Osceolas are only in Florida. The Rio Grande turkey is in the Southwest, and Merriam's turkeys are in the Rocky Mountain West. The Gould's turkey is in Arizona, New Mexico, and parts of Mexico.

Bird Dogs

Many bird hunters keep bird dogs to help them hunt. There are two main kinds of hunting dogs: pointers and retrievers. Pointers are especially good for upland bird hunting. They love running back and forth in a field, looking for the scent of a pheasant or a grouse or a partridge. Once they smell a bird, a good pointer will stand in one place, pointing with their nose toward the bird until the hunters arrive.

Retrievers are really good for waterfowl hunting. If you shoot a duck or a goose and it falls in icy water, a good retriever will have so much fun jumping in to fetch it back.

A good bird dog might start out as a kind of assistant. But as you hunt together and train and spend time in the field, the dog becomes something much more like a partner and very close friend.

Waterfowl

To waterfowl hunt, some hunters will throw out spreads of fake birds in a field or on the water, hoping to attract real birds. If ducks and geese see the decoys as they fly over, they might think there's something good to eat down there. Hopefully, they'll land and investigate. Some hunters will use duck or goose calls to help catch the birds' attention.

Every hunter has an idea about the best way to decoy. Some hunters will argue that you should place your fake birds in certain patterns on the ground. Others think that it doesn't matter a whole lot. If you're hunting snow geese, sometimes all you need are white bags spread around the ground! One thing's for sure, though: You should be well camouflaged yourself. Geese and ducks are really good at spotting hunters as they fly over.

Another way to hunt ducks and geese is by jump shooting. You walk along the riverbanks or creek bottoms. As the ducks or geese fly up from the water or gravel bars, startled, you might get a quick shot before they fly out of range.

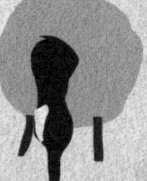

Sunrise

No matter whether you're hunting whitetails or turkeys, antelope or elk, you're probably going to have to get out of bed early to do it. Wild animals like sunrise and sunset—those times of the day when it's almost too dark to see. This is when they feel safest. Getting up early isn't much fun the first few times you do it, but eventually, you will come to appreciate these early mornings as the best parts of each day.

You wouldn't know it by watching the hunting shows on TV, but hunting is mostly walking and watching. For every minute you spend stalking and getting close to an animal, there are hours and hours spent just walking and glassing and thinking. After a while, you'll learn to appreciate how important walking and watching can be.

Seeing the sunrise or sunset all by yourself in the woods is one of the best reasons to go hunting.

Respect

After you kill your animal, it's very important that you treat it with respect. Another living creature has given its life so you can have something to eat. Please remember that. It's something that most of us, buying chicken at the grocery store or ordering hamburgers at the drive-through, have forgotten. In order for us to live, something else often has to die.

When you kill a big game animal, you will need to field dress it right away. Field dressing means you remove the stomach, intestines, lungs, and heart. This cools it off and keeps the meat from spoiling. It's not easy, though. The first few times you do it, you should probably plan on being taught by someone who already knows how it's done.

Ethical Hunting

In the early 1900s, many of the game animals that we take for granted now were almost gone. They were mostly killed off by unethical market hunters and by poachers. Unethical means that these hunters didn't care about how their actions affected other people or the animals they were hunting.

Luckily for us, sport hunters saw what was coming in time. They came together and agreed to limit the number of animals one person could kill. They also made hunting seasons and suggested that hunters should pay taxes to support habitat conservation. Even today, when you buy a gun or ammunition, part of the money you spend will help preserve the animals you're hunting.

In order to hunt, we need to take care of the wild animals and the places they live. The best hunters are also conservationists. They do what they can to preserve the natural world.

About the Author

A storyteller from way back, Allen Morris Jones has written eight other books, including the Spur-Award winning *Montana for Kids: the Story of Our State*, and *A Quiet Place of Violence: Hunting and Ethics in the Missouri River Breaks*. He's written some poetry, too. He and his wife live in Bozeman, Montana, with their teenage son.